Otto

Wagner

Otto Wagner

Otto Wagner

teNeues

Editor in chief:
Paco Asensio

Editor and original texts:
Sol Kliczkowski

Photographs:
© János Kalmár
Glassergasse 6, A-1090 Wien, Austria
info@janoskalmar.at

English translation:
William Bain

German translation:
Susanne Engler

French translation:
Thierry Lotte

Italian translation:
Giovanna Carnevali

Graphic Design / Layout:
Emma Termes Parera and Soti Mas-Bagà

Published worldwide by teNeues Publishing Group
(except Spain, Portugal and South-America):

teNeues Book Division
Neuer Zollhof 1, 40221 Düsseldorf, Germany
Tel: 0049-(0)211-994597-0
Fax: 0049-(0)211-994597-40

teNeues Publishing Company
16 West 22nd Street, New York, N.Y., 10010, USA
Tel.: 001-212-627-9090
Fax: 001-212-627-9511

teNeues Publishing UK Ltd.
Aldwych House, 71/91 Aldwych
London WC2B 4HN, UK
Tel.: 0044-1892-837-171
Fax: 0044-1892-837-272

teNeues France S.A.R.L.
140, rue de la Croix Nivert
75015 Paris, France
Tel.: 0033-1-5576-6205
Fax: 0033-1-5576-6419

www.teneues.com

Editorial project:

© 2002 LOFT Publications
Domènech 9, 2o 2a
08012 Barcelona, Spain
Tel.: 0034 932 183 099
Fax: 0034 932 370 060
e-mail: loft@loftpublications.com
www.loftpublications.com

Printed by:
Gráficas Anman. Sabadell, Spain.

September 2002

Die Deutsche Bibliothek – CIP-Einheitsaufnahme
Ein Titeldatensatz für diese Publikation ist bei der Deutschen Bibliothek erhältlic

ISBN: 3-8238-5545-X

Otto Wagner on his desk, engraving by Gottlieb Theodor Kempf Hartenkampf
Otto Wagner an seinem Schreibtisch, Gravur von Gottlieb Theodor Kempf Hartenkampf
Otto Wagner sur son bureau, gravure de Gottlieb Theodor Kempf Hartenkampf
Otto Wagner nella sua scrivania, incisione di Gottlieb Theodor Kempf Hartenkampf

The scientific discoveries of the end of the nineteenth century impacted on all artistic disciplines, and the city of Vienna took to the new trends in a daring spirit. Otto Wagner used the new knowledge in practical and theoretical ways and left his mark on modern architecture.

The legacy of the Viennese baroque, the Classical-Renaissance teachings Wagner received from teachers like Schinkel, Semper, or Theophil Hansen, combined with a pronounced innovative zeal, enabled him to aesthetically balance tradition and modernity.

Many emblematic names as Loos, Klimt, Hoffmann, Olbrich, Freud, Schiele, Kokoschka and Schönberg, some of them members of the Secession group, dot the landscape of fin-de-siècle Vienna. Most of these people participated in the changes from public institutions or from newspapers, as was the case with Wagner who, moreover, taught his anti-academic course at the Schillerplatz architectural school. At that point in time, modern architecture would come to form a part of official education, which conceded an enormous power to the school as an institution. It also afforded power to the new generations of architects, who would constitute the first workshop of modern architecture, prior even to that of Behrens. Its importance was such that without its alternative proposal the Secession would not have been conceivable.

Wagner's classes contained solid historical and technical groundings which he paralleled with the practical aspects of building. He favored a State promotion of art, laying special emphasis on the artist and their development. He would seek "a fair judgment of artistic feeling, correct and enthusiastic" (The Architecture Of Our Time, Vienna, 1914).

In his projects, Wagner did not fail to remember the perspective of the work as a whole, both in terms of the buildings and of the city itself. He was ever aware of the functional aspect. In the face of the agglomerative tendency in large city centers, he will propose a centrifugal expansion of the city and will achieve, in his artistic and functional involvement, a dilation of the metropolis effected with a certain order and harmony. His activity as a teacher and as an architect of large-scale works as the Viennese metro confer on him a signal place in fin-de-siècle Vienna.

Mutual influences between the Secessionists and Wagner are perceptible, although the latter would remain apart from the schematism of the movement and its rejection of the functionality he had always defended. Otto Wagner's career will culminate in the realization of his own architectural pieces, built according to his personal language.

Steinhof church, tint and aquarelle
Steinhof Kirche, Tusche und Aquarell
Église de Steinhof, encre et aquarelle
Chiesa de Steinhof, sfumatura e acquerello

Villa Wagner, tint and aquarelle
Villa Wagner, Tusche und Aquarell
Villa Wager, encre et aquarelle
Chiesa de Steinhof, sfumatura e acquerello

Die Entdeckungen der Wissenschaft gegen Ende des 19. Jahrhunderts wirkten sich auf alle künstlerischen Disziplinen aus, und vor allem in der Stadt Wien stand man den neuen und gewagten Strömungen sehr positiv gegenüber. Otto Wagner nahm diesen innovativen Geist in Theorie und Praxis auf und prägte so die moderne Architektur sehr stark.

Das Erbe des Wiener Barocks, die von der Klassik und Renaissance geprägte Bildung, die er von Professoren wie Schinkel, Semper oder Theophil Hansen erhielt, und das stete Streben nach Erneuerung ermöglichten es Wagner, ein ästhetisches Gleichgewicht zwischen der Tradition und der Moderne zu schaffen.

Viele emblematische Namen wie Loos, Klimt, Hoffmann, Olbrich, Freud, Schiele, Kokoschka und Schönberg, einige von ihnen Mitglieder der Künstlergruppe Secession, sind in Wien gegen Ende des 19. Jahrhunderts zu nennen. Die meisten dieser Künstler beeinflussten diese Veränderungen durch öffentliche Institutionen oder Zeitschriften. Das war auch bei Wagner der Fall, der außerdem seinen antiakademischen Unterricht in der Architekturschule Schillerplatz erteilte. Zu jener Zeit wurde die moderne Architektur Teil des offiziellen Unterrichts, was die Schule als Institution sehr stark werden ließ, und ebenso den neuen Generationen von Architekten, die zu jener ersten Werkstatt für moderne Architektur gehörten, die sogar schon vor Behrens existierte, enorme Kraft verlieh. Ihre Bedeutung war so groß, dass ohne diesen Alternativvorschlag die Secession niemals zustande gekommen wäre.

Wagner unterrichtete solide historische und technische Grundlagen, denen er parallel einen praktischen Aspekt beimischte. Er war ein Befürworter der staatlichen Förderung der Kunst, da diese dem Künstler in seiner Entwicklung eine besondere Bedeutung verleiht, und er forderte „eine Urteilskraft von treffsicherem und enthusiaschem Einfühlungsvermögen" („Die Baukunst unserer Zeit", Wien, 1914).

In seinen Projekten vergaß Wagner niemals den Gesamtheitsaspekt, und zwar in Bezug auf das Gebäude als auch auf die gesamte Stadt, und er legte stets einen besonderen Wert auf funktionelle Aspekte. Angesichts der Ballung großer städtischer Zentren schlug er eine zentrifugale Ausbreitung der Stadt vor, und erreichte durch seinen künstlerischen und funktionellen Eingriff, dass die Erweiterung der Metropole innerhalb einer gewissen Ordnung und Harmonie stattfand. Seiner Tätigkeit als Lehrer und als Architekt großer Bauwerke sowie der Untergrundbahn verdankte er eine besonders wichtige Position im Wien gegen Ende jenes Jahrhunderts.

Otto Wagner beteiligte sich an der Secession, aber er wusste auch, wann er sich aus dieser Bewegung zurückziehen musste, nämlich, als sie nur noch vom Schematismus geprägt war und immer mehr von der Funktionalität abkam, die er stets verteidigt hatte. Wagner konnte auf eine glänzende Laufbahn zurückblicken, die an seinen architektonischen Werken nachzuvollziehen ist, welche stets von seiner ganz persönlichen Sprache geprägt sind.

Suburban railway, drawing
Stadtbahn, Zeichnung
Métro, dessin
Ferrovia urbana, disegno

Les découvertes scientifiques de la fin du XIXème siècle eurent des conséquences dans toutes les disciplines artistiques, et Vienne accueillit les nouveaux courants avec audace. Otto Wagner se joignit corps et âme au nouvel esprit et laissa son empreinte dans l'architecture moderne.

L'héritage du Baroque Viennois et l'enseignement qu'il reçut sur le style Classique et Renaissance de professeurs comme Schinkel, Semper ou Theophil Hansen ainsi que son goût prononcé pour l'innovation permirent à Wagner de maintenir un équilibre esthétique entre tradition et modernité.

Beaucoup de figures emblématiques comme Loos, Klimt, Hoffmann, Olbrich, Freud, Schiele, Kokoschka et Schönberg, quelques'uns membres de le groupe Secession, marquèrent la Vienne de cette fin de siècle. La majorité d'entre eux deviendront les acteurs de ces changements, au travers d'institutions publiques ou d'organes de presse – comme Wagner – qui, de plus, dispensera un cours hors des normes académiques à l'école d'architecture de la Schillerplatz. C'est à cette époque que l'architecture moderne vint à faire partie de l'enseignement officiel ce qui conféra une grande force à l'école en tant qu'institution ainsi qu'aux nouvelles générations d'architectes qui constituèrent le premier atelier d'architecture moderne, avant même celui de Behrens. Son envergure fût telle, que sans cette proposition alternative le mouvement Secession n'aurait pas été concevable.

Wagner dispensa un enseignement basé sur de solides bases historiques et techniques en y mêlant parallèlement un aspect pratique ; il était partisan du mécénat d'état, et que ce dernier attache une importance particulière à l'artiste et à son évolution, en réclamant « un jugement de sensibilité artistique bien-fondé et enthousiaste » (« L'architecture de notre temps », Vienne, 1914).

Dans ses projets, Wagner ne perd pas de vue la perspective générale de l'ensemble : celle des immeubles en rapport avec celle de la cité et il se préoccupe toujours de leur côté pratique. Face au tassement des grands centres urbains, il propose une expansion centrifuge de la cité et réussit grâce à son intervention artistique et fonctionnelle que l'extension de la métropole soit poursuivie avec un certain ordre et de façon harmonieuse. Son activité en tant que professeur et architecte de grands travaux, comme la construction du métro, lui donne un rôle de premier plan dans la Vienne de cette fin de siècle.

Wagner participa au mouvement Secession et sut aussi s'en éloigner quand ce dernier prit un caractère schématique en s'éloignant de l'aspect fonctionnel qu'il avait toujours défendu. La trajectoire d'Otto Wagner atteint son point culminant et se manifeste dans les œuvres architecturales qu'il construit, fidèle à son langage personnel.

Linke Wienzeile building façade
Linke Wienzeile Gebäudefassade
Façade du bâtiment Linke Wienzeile
Facciata della costruzione Linke Wienzeile

Detail of the interior of the Neustiftgasse building
Innendetail des Gebäudes in der Neustiftgasse
Détail du intérieur du bâtiment de la Neustiftgasse
Detaglio interiore dell'edificio della Neustiftgasse

Le scoperte scientifiche della fine del secolo XIX si ripercossero in tutte le discipline artistiche, e la città di Vienna accolse le nuove correnti con audacia. Otto Wagner si impersonificò sia a livello teorico che pratico a questo nuovo spirito che stavasorgendo e lasciò una traccia nella architettura moderna.

L'eredità del Baroccco Viennese e gli insegnamenti classico-rinascimentali che ricevette da professori di un certo calibro come Schinkel, Semper o Theophil Hansen uniti a un grande desiderio di innovazione, permisero a Wagner di mantenersi sempre in un costante equilibrio estetico tra tradizione e modernità.

Molti uomini emblematici, come Loos, Klimt, Hoffmann, Olbrich, Freud, Schiele, Kokoschka e Schönberg, alcuni di loro membri del gruppo Secession, acquistano notorietà nella Vienna del fine secolo. La maggior parte di questi partecipano alle grandi trasformazioni a partire dai cambi delle istituzioni pubbliche a quelle dei quotidiani, come per esempio Wagner, che inoltre, impartisce un corso accademico presso la facoltà di architettura Schillerplatz. In questo periodo l'architettura moderna entrò a fare parte della didattica ufficiale, e questo conferisce un incredibile prestigio alla scuola come istituzione e alle nuove generazioni di architetti che costituiranno il primo laboratorio di architettura moderna, anteriore a quello di Behrens. Anche se non coincise con la Secession, la sua proposta fu altrettanto aperta e diffusa.

Wagner diede lezioni di solidi fondamenti storici e tecnici ai quali unì anche l'aspetto pratico; era un sostenitore del patrocinio statale dell'arte in quanto consistevca nell'accreditare una speciale importanza all'artista durante la propia evoluzione, e questo richiedeva "un giudizio di sensibilità artistica accertata e entusiasta" ("L'architettura del nostro tempo", Vienna, 1914).

Nei suoi progetti Wagner non si dimentica della prospettiva dell'insieme, sia degli edifici così come della città, e si preoccupa sempre dell'aspetto fuzionale. Invece di proporre progetti basati sul concetto di agglomerazione urbana, preferisce pensare a un'espansione centrifuga della città e raggiunge l'obiettivo mediante il suo apporto artistico e funzionale dove la metropoli ottiene la sua identità con un certo ordine e armonia. La sua attività come professore e come architetto, di grandi opere come ad esempio la costruzione del metro, gli conferiscono una posizione distaccata, di prestigio nella Vienna del fine secolo.

Otto Wagner partecipò al movimento della Secession ed ebbe la capacità di capire quando ritirarsi, ossia nel momento in cui stava aquisendo schematismi e si distaccava dalla funzionalità di sempre che aveva difeso. Il percorso di formazione di Wagner culmina e si manifesta nelle sue opere architettoniche, che rappresentano fedelmente il suo linguaggio personale.

Länderbank

Hohenstaufengasse 3, Vienna, Austria
1884

This work to a great extent determines the beginning of a new phase of Otto Wagner's architecture. What the architect inherits from classicism may be glimpsed here, yet there is also an introduction of modern techniques and new materials. The building methods stand out, moreover, for their functionalism and for the elegance with which the piece resolves its spatial organization. The architect thus uses the praxis contained in one of his sentences: "It cannot be beautiful if it is not practical." (The Architecture Of Our Time). From the outside, the building's façade is clearly traditional and does not reflect the interior structure. Set on an irregularly shaped site, the bank has been projected by the architect on a circular plan. The vestibule thus becomes the main axis of the whole mass. Abstract Austria, sculpted by Johannes Benk, echoes this circular arrangement in the statue's placement at the junction with the main room. The lobby then suggests a Tuscan order, with a play of columns alternating round pilasters with square ones and a lantern roof of iron and glass, reflecting one of the technological advances of the nineteenth century.

Dieses Werk war bestimmend für den Beginn einer neuen Etappe in der Architektur Otto Wagners. Man kann noch das klassische Erbe erkennen, aber er führte hier moderne Techniken und neue Materialien ein. Das Gebäude hebt sich außerdem aufgrund seiner Funktionalität und der Eleganz hervor, mit der die Aufteilung des Raums durchgeführt wurde. Der Architekt setzte dabei eine seiner Überzeugungen in die Praxis um: „Was nicht praktisch ist, kann auch nicht schön sein", erklärte er in seinem Buch „Die Baukunst unserer Zeit". Von außen betrachtet weist das Gebäude eine traditionelle Fassade auf, an der man die innere Struktur nicht erkennen kann. Das Gebäude wurde auf einem unebenen Gelände errichtet, auf dem der Architekt eine kreisförmige Anordnung entwarf. Aus dem Vestibül wird so die Hauptachse des Gebäudes. Für den Anschluss an den Hauptsaal wurde eine kreisförmige Achse benutzt, auf der ein Standbild des Künstlers Johannes Benk aufgestellt wurde, das das Land Österreich verkörpert. Im Publikumssaal spielte er mit den Säulen auf den toskanischen Stil an: Pilaster mit rundem Säulenschaft wechseln sich mit quadratischen Säulen ab. An der Decke befindet sich ein Dachfenster aus Eisen und Glas, eine Konstruktion, die durch den technologischen Fortschritt im 19. Jahrhundert möglich wurde.

Cette œuvre détermine en grande partie le début d'une période dans l'architecture d'Otto Wagner : on entrevoit encore l'héritage du classique, mais il introduit déjà la Modernité dans les techniques et utilise de nouveaux matériaux. La construction se distingue en outre par sa fonctionnalité et par l'élégance avec laquelle elle résout l'organisation de l'espace. L'architecte met ainsi en pratique une de ses devises : « Ce qui n'est pas pratique ne peut pas être beau » ainsi qu'il le précisera dans son livre « L'Architecture de notre temps ». De l'extérieur on remarque que la façade de l'édifice est traditionnelle et ne reflète pas sa structure intérieure. La construction s'appuie sur un terrain irrégulier sur lequel, l'architecte a projeté une articulation circulaire. Le hall devient ainsi l'axe principal du volume. Pour faire la jonction avec la salle principale on a utilisé un axe circulaire où l'on a placé une statue de L'Autriche sculptée par Johannes Benk. Le hall de réception du public suggère un ordre dans le style Toscan avec un jeu de colonnes qui fait alterner pilastres de bois ronds avec des colonnes carrées et il est surmonté par une verrière de fer et de verre, témoin des progrès technologiques du XIXème siècle.

Questa opera determina in grandi linee il principio una tappa dell'architettura di Otto Wagner: si intravede una certa eredità classica ma al tempo stesso introduce la modernità delle tecniche e dei materiali nuovi. Il suo modo di costruire si distacca inoltre per la sua funzionalità e per l'eleganza attraverso cui risolve l'organizzazione dello spazio. L'architetto commenta in una delle sue sentenze: "No può essere bello ciò che non é pratico", concetto che elaborerà successivamente nel suo libro "L'architettura del nostro tempo". Dall'esterno si può osservare che la facciata dell'edificio é tradizionale e non riflette la struttura interna. La costruzione si organizza su un terreno irregolare su cui l'architetto progettò un'articolazione circolare. L'entrata si converte quindi nell'asse principale di questo volume. Per l'unione con la sala principale, venne utilizzato un asse circolare dove si collocò una statua dell'Austria scolpita da Johannes Benk. La sala del pubblico suggerisce un ordine toscano con un gioco di colonne che alterna colonne dal fusto rotondo con quelle di base quadrata, e sono coperte da un lucernario fatto in ferro e vetro, riflesso del progresso tecnologico del XIX° secolo.

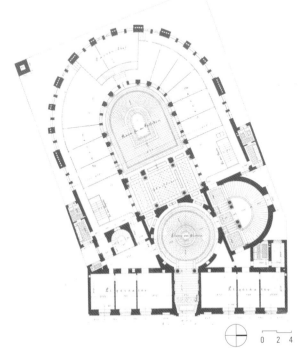

Ground floor
Erdgeschoss
Rez-de-chaussée
Piano terra

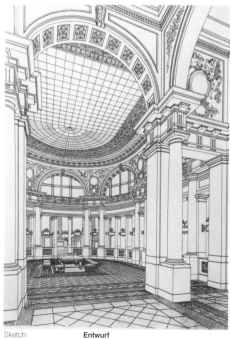

Sketch   **Entwurf**

Esquisse   **Schizzo**

Wagner's Villas

Hüttelbergstraße 26/Hüttelbergstraße 28,
Vienna, Austria
1886/1912–1913

The first of the Wagner Villas is a house in the classical tradition. Otto Wagner built it as a summer residence after he married for the second time. One salient feature is its great symmetry; another is the innovative use of the iron in the railings of the staircase. The house is on a square plan with a transversal axis with two galleries. The entrance has a long portico with four columns. Essentially made of stone, the galleries include windows of stained glass. The second villa exhibits a great creative capacity: freedom in the rooms, geometrical decoration and asymmetry in the entrance and the gallery. Wagner goes beyond the established architecture (influenced largely by Loos and Hoffmann), marking his use of blue and white majolica tiles. He gives special importance to the entrance and strongly states his own presence with a plastic work in the small window decorated by Kolo Moser. In comparing the two villas, one appreciates the architect's development, which comes to include a renunciation of all style in the second piece, the last and most modern of his works.

Die erste der von ihm erbauten Villen ist ein klassisch geprägtes Wohnhaus. Otto Wagner errichtete sie als Sommerwohnsitz nach seiner zweiten Heirat. Sie zeichnet sich durch Symmetrie und innovative Elemente wie das Eisengitter am Treppengeländer aus. Es handelt sich um ein Gebäude mit einem quadratischen Grundriss mit schräg verlaufender Achse und zwei Galerien. Der Zugang erfolgt über eine Säulenhalle, die von vier Säulen mit einem Türfenster getragen wird. Beim Bau wurde vor allem Stein verwendet, und die Galerien sind mit dekorierten Glasfenstern geschmückt. In der zweiten Villa brachte der Architekt seine große Kreativität zum Ausdruck. Auffallend ist die Freiheit der Raumaufteilung, die geometrische Dekoration und die Asymmetrie des Eingangs und der Galerie. Wagner setzte sich über die traditionelle Architektur hinweg, wobei er in großem Maße von Loos und Hoffmann beeinflusst wurde. Als Dekoration benutzte er beispielsweise blaue und weiße Majolikakacheln. Besonderen Wert legte der Architekt auf den Eingangsbereich und betonte diesen mit einer Skulptur in dem kleinen Fenster, die von Kolo Moser geschaffen wurde. Wenn man beide Gebäude vergleicht, erkennt man die Entwicklung des Architekten, der bei dem zweiten Wohnhaus, dem letzten und modernsten seiner Werke, auf jegliche Stilisierung verzichtete.

La première villa constitue une résidence avec des apports venus de la tradition classique. Wagner l'a construite comme résidence d'été après son second mariage. C'est son aspect symétrique qui ressort principalement ; on note pourtant des innovations dans la grille d'entrée en fer forgé. Il s'agit de la construction d'un volume sur plan carré avec un axe transversal à deux galeries. L'accès en est un portique soutenu par quatre colonnes avec une porte-fenêtre. On a utilisé essentiellement de la pierre et les galeries ont été recouvertes de verrières décorées. Dans la seconde villa, on peut apprécier une grande capacité créatrice : liberté d'espaces, décoration géométrique et asymétrique de l'entrée et de la galerie. Wagner réussit à surpasser l'architecture de son temps – influencée en grande partie par Loos et Hoffmann – en utilisant comme ornementation des azulejos émaillés (majoliques) bleus et blancs. L'architecte attribue une importance particulière à l'entrée et souligne sa présence par une œuvre plastique dans la petite fenêtre décorée par Kolo Moser. En comparant les deux œuvres on peut noter l'évolution de l'architecte qui finit par renoncer à toute forme de style dans la seconde résidence, la dernière et la plus moderne de ses œuvres.

La prima casa costituisce una residenza con riferimenti alla tradizione classica. Wagner la costruì come dimora estiva dopo il suo secondo matrimonio. Si riconosce una grande simmetria; non ostante tutto si apprezzano le innovazioni nel cancello di ferro e nelle ringhiere delle scale. Si tratta di un volume a pianta cuadrata con un asse traversale con due gallerie. L'ingresso é costituito da un porticato di quattro colonne con una porta-finestra. Si utilizzò fondamentalmente la pietra e le gallerie vennero coperte da vetrate variopinte. Nella seconda casa si apprezza molto la sua capacità creativa: libertà negli spazi, decorazione geometrica e asimmetrica dell'entrata e della galleria. Wagner riesce a superare l'architettura consolidata – quella che influenza in gran parte Loos e Hoffmann – utilizzando come ornamento, con una certa sobrietà, piastrelle di mayolica azzurri e bianche. L'architetto conferisce molta importanza all'entrata e marca la sua presenza mediante un'opera plastica incarnata nella piccola finestra decorata da Kolo Moser. Nel confronto di entrambe le opere si può apprezzare l'evoluzione dell'architetto che giunge nel rinuciare a tutto lo stile nella seconda residenza, l'ultima e la più moderna delle sue opere.

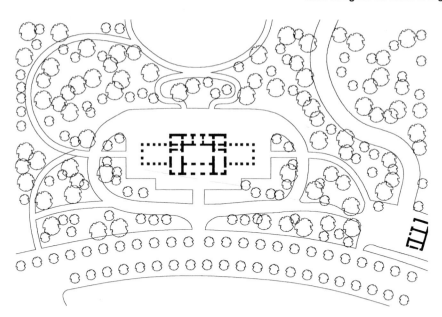

Plan
Grundriss
Niveau
Pianta

0 10 20

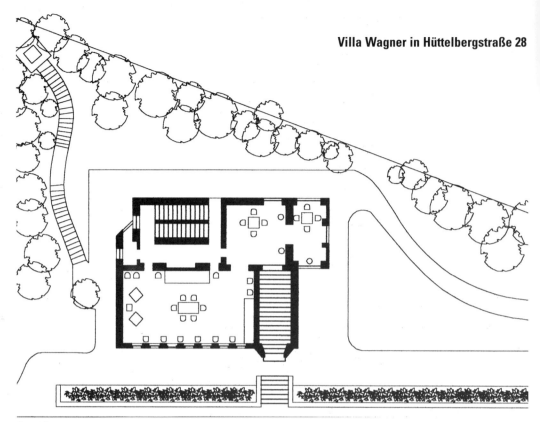

Villa Wagner in Hüttelbergstraße 28

Ground floor
Erdgeschoss
Rez-de-chaussée
Piano terra

0 1 2

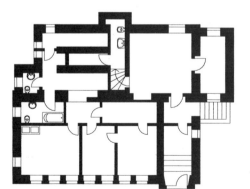

Basement
Souterrain
Sous-sole
Piano interrato

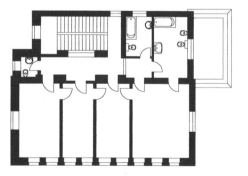

First floor
Erstes Obergeschoss
Premier étage
Primo piano

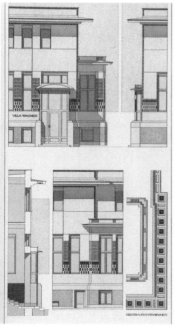

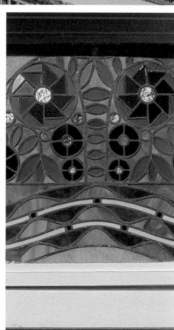

Majolica House

Linke Wienzeile 40, Vienna, Austria
1898–1899

With this residence, Wagner opens himself to the movement of the young artists of the age at a crowning moment of his fame: along with another house on the same street (Linke Wienzeile Building 38), he thus provokes the disapproval of the Künstlerhaus conservatives. The façade of the Majolica House is distinct from that of the adjacent house (also by Wagner) because of the building's pink floral whirls printed on majolica tiles – hence the name – and the lions framing the windows. The floors of the two buildings are not in alignment but are joined by a series of balconies that are set back from the front. It is by these means that the Majolica House presents its façade flanked by two "columns" of balconies. Inside, the staircase, which houses an elegant elevator decorated in the Secessionist style, governs the vertical axis, interrupted by the short passageways of each mezzanine floor. For the whole length of the stairway, the curved lines and the design of the elevator housing and of the staircase handrail live up to the creativity of the young Secessionist movement.

Mit diesem Wohnhaus öffnete sich Wagner für die Bewegung junger Künstler der Epoche in einem Augenblick, in dem er den Gipfel seiner Karriere erreicht hatte. Zusammen mit einem anderen Haus in der gleichen Straße erregte es bei den konservativen Mitgliedern des Künstlerhauses große Missbilligung. Die Fassade dieses Hauses unterscheidet sich von der Nachbarfassade, die ebenfalls von Otto Wagner stammt, durch die Dekoration mit rosa Blumengirlanden, die auf die Majolikakacheln gedruckt sind (daher der Name), und durch die Löwen, die das Fenster umrahmen. Die Stockwerke des Gebäudes befinden sich nicht auf einer Linie, werden aber durch die Säulen der hinteren Balkone der Fassade vereint. Deshalb hat das Majolikahaus eine Fassade, die von den zwei Säulen der Balkone flankiert wird. Im Inneren bestimmt das Treppenhaus, in dem sich ein eleganter, im Secessionsstil dekorierter Fahrstuhl befindet, die Vertikalität des Gebäudes, die von zwei kurzen Fluren in jedem Zwischengeschoss unterbrochen wird. An der gesamten Treppe entlang zeigen die kurvenförmigen Linien und die Entwürfe des Gitterwerks des Fahrstuhls sowie des Treppengeländers die Kreativität der jungen Secessionsbewegung.

Avec cette résidence, Wagner s'ouvre au mouvement des jeunes artistes de l'époque au moment où il atteint sa plus grande célébrité, et, avec une autre maison construite dans la même rue, il provoque le désaveu des conservateurs de la Künstlerhaus. La façade de cette maison se distingue de sa voisine (également de Otto Wagner) par son décor de tourbillons de fleurs roses plaquées sur des azulejos émaillés (origine du nom Majolique) et par les têtes de lions qui encadrent les fenêtres. Les étages des deux constructions ne sont pas alignés mais s'unissent par une colonne de balcons plus en retrait par rapport aux façades. C'est la raison pour laquelle la Maison des Majoliques présente en façade deux colonnes de balcons qui encadrent l'édifice. A l'intérieur, la cage d'escalier abrite un élégant ascenseur décoré dans le style « Secession », qui divise la verticalité de l'édifice en l'interrompant par de petits couloirs qui signalent chaque entresols. Tout le long de l'escalier, les lignes courbes et le dessin du grillage de l'ascenseur ainsi que de la rampe d'escalier nous font admirer la créativité du jeune mouvement « Sezession ».

Con questa casa, Wagner si apre al movimento dei giovani artisti dell'epoca, coincidendo nel momento della sua massima notorietà; e insieme all'altra residenza nella stessa strada, genera scontento e disapprovazione da parte dei conservatori della Künstlerhaus. La facciata di questa casa si distingue da quella attigua, sempre di Otto Wagner, grazie alla decorazione fatta con vortici floreali di colore rosa impressi sulle piatrelle di majolica (da qui il suo nome) e grazie ai leoni che marcano le finestre. Le piante dei due edifici non sono allineate ma si uniscono mediante a una colonna di balconi che si trova arretrata rispetto alle facciate. In questo modo, la Casa della Mayolica presenta la sua facciata fiancheggiata da due colonne di balconi che evidenziano l'edificio. All'interno, il blocco scale dove alberga un elegante ascensore decorato secondo lo stile secessionista, quest'ultimo mette in evidenza la verticalità dell'edificio che viene interrotta da corti corridoi di ciascuna delle piante intermedie. Lungo tutta la scala, le linee curve e il disegno della griglia dell'ascensore e delle ringhiere dimostrano creatività del giovane movimento della Secession.

The Linke Wienzeile Building 38

Linke Wienzeile 38, Vienna, Austria
1898–1899

Beside the Majolica House, Otto Wagner raised this house on the Linke Wienzeile (originally called Magdalenenstraße). The two buildings are very striking owing to their ornamental façades, and this one is decorated in gilded stucco. The facings were commissioned to Kolo Moser, the artist and founding member of the Secession. The rich decoration in cascades, leaf motifs, and medallions bearing women's faces covers the façade and contrasts with the floral motifs on the neighboring block. Later, both artists would collaborate on the Steinhof Church. The commercial space behind the display windows on the ground floor lighten the weight of the whole. The first floor is joined to the second by way of staffs that are projected upward. Wagner paid special attention to the design of the "rounded corner", which has three windows per floor. Crowning this are two bronze sculptures by Othmar Schimkowitz. As in the Majolica House, great care was taken in the internal details – staircase, elevator, handrail – to mark the social status of the people who would live here.

Otto Wagner erbaute dieses Wohnhaus neben dem Majolikahaus in der Linken Wienzeile, die vorher Magdalenenstraße hieß. Diese beiden benachbarten Gebäude lenken aufgrund ihrer geschmückten Fassaden die Aufmerksamkeit der Passanten auf sich. Der goldene Stuck dieser Fassade wurde von Kolo Moser ausgeführt, einem Künstler, der Gründungsmitglied der Secession war. Die kaskadenförmige Dekoration, das Laubwerk und die Medaillons mit dem Antlitz einer Frau ziehen sich über die Vorderfront und bilden einen Kontrast zu den Blumenmotiven des Nachbargebäudes. Später arbeiteten beide Künstler an der Kirche „Am Steinhof" zusammen. Die Schaufensterscheiben der Geschäftsräume im Erdgeschoss vermindern die Schwere des Gebäudes. Das erste Stockwerk wird durch aufstrebende Binder mit dem zweiten vereint. Besonderen Wert hatte Wagner auf die Ausführung der „abgerundeten Ecke" gelegt, an der sich in jedem Stockwerk drei Fenster befinden. Diese Straßenecke wird von zwei Bronzefiguren gekrönt, die von Othmar Schimkowitz geschaffen wurden. Ebenso wie bei dem Majolikahaus sind die Einzelheiten im Inneren wie Treppe, Fahrstuhl und Geländer mit großer Sorgfalt ausgearbeitet. So wird die gesellschaftliche Stellung der künftigen Bewohner noch unterstrichen.

Otto Wagner construisit cette résidence à coté de la Maison des Majoliques dans la rue Linke Wienzeile, anciennement appelée Magdalenenstraße. Les deux constructions, contiguës, attirent l'attention des passants par leurs façades ornementales. Dans cette construction, la façade est en stuc doré et elle fut commandée à Kolo Moser, artiste et membre fondateur du mouvement « Sezession ». La décoration en cascades, les feuillages et les médaillons à visages de femme parcourent le front de l'édifice et contrastent avec les motifs floraux de l'immeuble voisin. Plus tard, les deux artistes collaborèrent tous les deux à l'église de Steinhof. L'espace commercial vitré du rez-de-chaussée allège le poids de l'ensemble ; le premier étage communique avec le second par colonettes métalliques verticales. Wagner fit particulièrement attention au profil de « l'angle arrondi » qui présente trois fenêtres à chaque étage. Pour couronner ce pan coupé on y plaça deux sculptures de bronze de Othmar Schimkowitz. A l'instar de la Maison des Majoliques, on a soigné particulièrement les détails intérieurs – escalier, cage d'ascenseur et rampe de l'escalier – de façon à bien marquer le statut social des futurs habitants.

Otto Wagner costruì questo edificio per residenze insieme alla Casa di Mayólica nella via Linke Wienzeile, anticamente chiamata Magdalenenstraße. I due edifici contigui, richiamano l'attenzione del passante per le loro facciate ornamentate. Questo é un edificio in stucco dorato, incarico dato a Kolo Moser, artista e membro fondatore della Secession. La decorazione in cascate e fogliame e trofei rappresentati volti femminili si ricorrono in facciata e contrastano con i motivi floreali del blocco vivino. Successivamente entrambi gli artisti collaboreranno insieme per la chiesa di Steinhof. Lo spazio commerciale vetrato in pianta bassa alleggerisce il peso al congiunto; il primo piano si connette al secondomediante aste che si proiettano in senso ascendente. Wagner ebbe speciale attenzione per il disegno "dell'angolo arrotondato", dove presenta tre finestre per ciascun piano. A conclusione della superficie obliqua si collocarono due figure di bronzo scolpite da Othmar Schimkowitz. Come per a Casa di Mayólica, si curarono con estrema attenzione i dettagli degli interni – scala, ascensore, e ringhiera – sottolineando così lo stato sociale della gente che la sarebbe andata ad abitare.

Vienna Metro Stations

Vienna, Austria
1894–1901

The Stadtbahn (Metropolitan Railway) was Wagner's first commission after he was named official adviser for the construction of the Vienna Town Hall in 1894. The stations would be gradually inserted into the urban landscape to adapt themselves to the buildings around them. This is clear if we look at the different stations over the course of the line's growth, like Gersthof or Rossauer Lände. The different stations are linkers that inexorably mark Vienna's city landscape and transport their design in the direction of the U-bahn/S-bahn system. The structure will vary according to whether the rails are elevated or subterranean, but throughout the system what predominates is the use of iron painted in green and an enormous wealth of technical solutions. This confirms the path acquired by the architecture and its connection to Art Nouveau. In any case, classical inspiration can hardly be said to disappear either: it is transformed and adapts the use-oriented ideal and the clarity of modern times.

Die U-Bahn war der erste Auftrag, der Wagner nach seiner Ernennung zum Künstlerischen Beirat der Wiener Kommission für Verkehrsanlagen und Donauregulierung im Jahre 1894 erteilt wurde. Die Bahnhöfe fügen sich in die Stadtlandschaft ein und passen sich an die Gebäude der Umgebung an, wie an den Bahnhöfen Gersthof oder Rossauer Lände gut zu erkennen ist. Die verschiedenen Pavillons stellen ein Verbindungselement dar, das zweifelsohne die Stadtlandschaft von Wien stark geprägt hat, und sie tragen ihr Design bis zu den Stationen am Stadtrand. Die Struktur verändert sich, je nachdem, ob es sich um eine oberirdische oder eine unterirdische Linie handelt. Bei allen jedoch dominiert die Verwendung von grün gestrichenem Eisen und eine große Vielfalt an technischen Lösungen, welche die künstlerische Ausrichtung des Architekten und seine Verbindung zur Art Nouveau bestätigen. Dennoch verschwindet die klassische Inspiration niemals, sie wird umgewandelt und an das Funktionalitätsideal und die Klarheit der modernen Zeiten angepasst.

Le métro fût la première commande que reçut Wagner après sa nomination comme conseiller supérieur pour la construction à la mairie de Vienne en 1894. Les stations s'insèrent dans le paysage urbain en s'adaptant aux constructions ambiantes ; c'est ce que l'on peut constater à la station de Gersthof ou bien à celle de Rossauer Lände. Les différentes bouches de métro sont un fil conducteur qui marque indubitablement le paysage de Vienne et leur design se retrouve dans les petites gares qui entourent la ville. Leur structure diffère selon la ligne – aérienne ou souterraine – mais toutes ont un point commun : l'emploi du fer forgé peint en vert et une énorme richesse de solutions techniques, ce qui confirme la direction prise par l'architecture et son lien avec l'Art Nouveau. De toute façon l'inspiration classique ne disparaît pas : elle se transforme et s'adapte à l'idéal fonctionnel et à la clarté des temps modernes.

Il metro fu il primo incarico che Wagner ricevette dopo la sua nomina come consigliere superiore per la costruzione del Comune di Vienna nel 1894. Le stazioni si inseriscono nel paesaggio urbano adattandosi agli edifici attigui; solo in questo modo si possono apprezzare le stazioni di Gersthof o di Rossauer Lände. I differenti padiglioni sono un elemento di cogiunzione che sottolinea inevitabilmente il paesaggio della città di Vienna e trasporta la sua linea verso le piccole stazioni che circondano la città. La struttura varia a seconda se sono per la linea sopraelevata o per quella sotterranea, anche se in tutte le stazioni predomina l'uso del ferro colorato di verde e un'enorme ricchezza nelle soluzioni tecniche, confermando l'impostazione che aquisisce l'architettura e il suo voncolo all'Art Nouveau. In ogni caso l'ispirazione classica non scompare, si trasforma e si adatta all'ideale di chiarezza e funzionalità dei tempi moderni.

Station Friedensbrücke
Station Friedensbrücke
Station de Friedensbrücke
Stazione di Friedensbrücke

Station Hütteldorf-Hacking (previous page)
Station Hütteldorf-Hacking (vorherige Seite)
Station de Hütteldorf-Hacking (page précédente)
Stazione di Hütteldorf-Hacking (pagina precedente)

Service building for Danube River canal navigation
Dienstgebäude für die Schifffahrt auf dem Donaukanal
Pavillon des services de navigation sur le canal du Danube
Padiglione dei servizi della navigazione nel canale del Danubio

Station Nussdorfer Straße (previous page)
Station Nussdorfer Straße (vorherige Seite)
Station de Nussdorfer Straße (page précédente)
Stazione di Nussdorfer Straße (pagina precedente)

Hofpavillon

Schönbrunn, Austria
1898

Otto Wagner thought that the imperial court required a metro station for its exclusive use in the summer residence of Schönbrunn, in the Wien River valley. He thus drew up plans for the Hofpavillon, an imperial style piece that does not follow the basic paradigms on which the rest of the stations are built. Instead, Hofpavillon provided the opportunity for him to demonstrate to the emperor the triumph of the codes of modern art. There is a luxurious waiting room finished in silk and mahogany. The interior includes a large view of Vienna from close to ten thousand feet (three thousand meters) by Carl Moll, with two royal eagles in the foreground and the different metropolitan railway lines. The outside view shows a plain structure with such architectural decorative details as oval windows in the dome. It is also adorned with consoles and medallions that have acquired a green patina owing to oxidation. The metal marquee with gilt elements was used so that court guests could be protected as they waited in carriages that would take them to the castle.

Otto Wagner war der Ansicht, dass der Kaiserhof über eine eigene U-Bahn-Station an der Sommerresidenz Schönbrunn verfügen sollte, die sich im Wienfluss-Tal befindet. Deshalb entwarf er die Haltestelle Hofpavillon im Kaiserstil, die nicht dem grundlegenden Modell der übrigen Haltestellen entspricht, aber mit der er dem Kaiser den Siegeszug der modernen Kunst vorführen konnte. Es handelt sich um einen luxuriösen Wartesaal, der mit Seide und Mahagoni dekoriert ist. In seinem Inneren hängt eine große Ansicht von Wien aus dreitausend Metern Höhe, ausgeführt von Carl Moll, mit zwei Kaiseradlern im Vordergrund und den verschiedenen U-Bahn-Strecken. Die nüchtern wirkende, äußere Struktur wird durch dekorative, architektonische Einzelheiten wie die ovalen Fenster, welche die Kuppel umgeben, aufgelockert, und ist mit Konsolen und Medaillons verziert, die mittlerweile durch die Einwirkung der Luft auf das Metall eine grünliche Farbe angenommen haben. Hinter den Metallmarkisen mit aufgemalten goldenen Elementen konnten die Gäste des Hofes geschützt auf die Karossen warten, die sie zum Schloss brachten.

Otto Wagner pensait que la cour impériale devait avoir une station de métro à son usage exclusif dans sa résidence estivale de Schönbrunn, située dans la vallée du fleuve de Vienne. C'est ainsi qu'il fit le projet du Hofpavillon, un volume de style empire qui ne suit pas les modèles communs aux autres gares, mais qui lui donnait l'occasion de démontrer à l'empereur les atouts des codes esthétiques de l'art moderne. Il s'agit d'une luxueuse salle d'attente tendue de soie et d'acajou. A l'intérieur pend une grande vue de Vienne prise à trois mille mètres d'altitude, réalisée par Carl Moll, avec deux aigles impériaux au premier plan et les différents trajets du métro. L'aspect extérieur présente une structure sobre avec des détails décoratifs architecturaux comme les fenêtres ovales qui entourent la coupole, cette dernière ornée de consoles et de médaillons qui ont pris une couleur verdâtre due à l'action corrosive de l'atmosphère sur le métal. La marquise métallique avec dorures servait à ce que les hôtes de la Cour attendent à l'abri les carrosses qui devaient les conduire au château.

Otto Wagner pensò che la corte imperiale dovesse avere una propria stazione del metro per uso esclusivo nella residenza estiva di Schönbrunn, situata nella valle del fiume Wien. Fu così che progettò il Hofpavillon, un volume in stile imperiale che non segue i modelli basi di tutte le altre stazioni, e gli premise di dimostrare all'imperatore il trionfo dei codici dell'arte moderna. Si tratta di un lussuoso salone d'attesa rivestito di seta e mogano. Al suo interno é appesa una grande veduta di Vienna realizzata a tre mila metri d'altezza, opera di Carl Moll, con due aquile reali in primo piano e le diverse linee del metro. L'esterno si presenta come una struttura sobria con dettagli decorativi architettonici come le finestre ovali che circondano la cupola, quest'ultima adornata da mensole e trofei que hanno aquisito un colre verde a causa dell'azione atmosferica sul metallo. La copertura in metallo con elementi decorativi dipinti era utilizzata dagli ospiti alla corte reale come tettoia sotto cui ripararsi in caso di pioggia al fine di raggiungere in carrozza il castello.

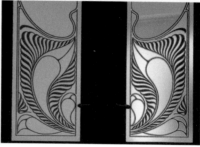

Karlsplatz

Karlsplatz, Vienna, Austria
1898

Wagner built the Karlsplatz station using two pavilions in accord with the idea that its grandeur would match that of the two Habsburg residences, the city home of Hofburg, and the summer one of Schönbrunn. Unlike the other stations, these employ a self-supporting panel structure on iron faced in white marble. The interior panels are not marble, but plaster. The initial project foresaw a dome to crown the station, but after the final approbation was given for the square – one of the most important in Vienna – its construction was rejected and the station entrances received more functional treatment as symbols of modernity. The whole was decorated according to Secessionist design concepts, which also contributed to this innovative standard. On this project, the architect combined to advantage the liveliness of the colors with the abundance of Art Nouveau motifs. Colors, in fact, alternate with gilt in the decorations and the white and green of the framework.

Wagner erbaute für die Station Karlsplatz zwei Pavillons, wobei er von der Idee geleitet wurde, dass ihre große Pracht mit den beiden Residenzen der Habsburger in Verbindung stehen müsse, mit der Stadtresidenz Hofburg und der Sommerresidenz Schönbrunn. Im Gegensatz zu den anderen Stationen bestehen diese aus einer selbsttragenden Tafelstruktur, die auf Eisen montiert und mit weißen Marmorplatten außen und Gipsplatten innen verkleidet ist. Ursprünglich war eine Kuppel vorgesehen, welche die Station krönen sollte. Aber nachdem der endgültige Entwurf für den Platz, der einer der wichtigsten in Wien ist, angenommen wurde, wurde von der Konstruktion der Kuppel abgesehen, denn die Pavillons sollten ein Symbol für die Modernität darstellen. Der Komplex wurde im Secessionsstil dekoriert, was ebenfalls zu dieser innovativen Atmosphäre beitrug. Bei diesem Bau kombinierte der Architekt gekonnt die Lebhaftigkeit der Farben mit der Fülle an Motiven der Art Nouveau. Die Farben wechseln sich mit Goldtönen in den Dekorationen ab, und die Farben Weiß und Grün wurden in der Struktur verwendet.

Wagner construisit pour la station de Karlsplatz deux pavillons en accord avec l'idée que dans leur grande somptuosité ils assureraient l'union avec les deux résidences des Habsbourgs, celle de Vienne – la Hofburg – et celle d'été – Schönbrunn. Contrairement aux autres stations, ces dernières présentent une structure de panneaux autoportants montés sur fer et revêtus avec des plaques de marbre blanc sur la face extérieure et de plaques de plâtre sur la face intérieure. Le projet initial prévoyait une coupole qui surmontait la gare, mais après approbation du plan final de la place – une des plus emblématiques de Vienne – on refusa sa construction – de façon à ce que les pavillons soient construits comme un symbole de la modernité. L'ensemble fût décoré selon un dessin « secessioniste » ce qui contribua aussi à créer cette ambiance innovatrice. Dans ce projet, l'architecte sût combiner la vivacité des couleurs avec l'abondance des motifs Art Nouveau ; les couleurs alternent avec les dorures des motifs décoratifs et le blanc et le vert dominent toute la structure.

Wagner costruì due padiglioni per la stazione di Karlsplatz, in accordo con l'idea che la sua magnificenza si mantenesse insieme alle due residenze degli Absburgo, con quella della città – Hofburg – e con quella estiva – Schönbrunn. A differenza delle altre stazioni, queste presentano una struttura in pannelli autoportanti montati su ferro e rivestiti con placche di marmo bianco nella parte esetriore, mentre per quella interiore in gesso. Il progetto iniziale prevedeva una cupola che coronasse la stazione, ma durante la fase di approvazione del disegno generale della piazza – una delle più significative di Vienna –, si scartò a favore del fatto che i padiglioni si erigessero come simbolo della modernità. Tutto l'insieme venne decorato secondo il disegno secessionista, che contribuì a generare questo disegno innovativo. In questo progetto, l'architetto seppe combinare la vivacità dei colori con l'abbondanza dei motivi ornamentali dell'Art Nouveau; i colori si alternano con i dorati nelle decorazioni mentre il bianco e il verde viene usato per la struttura.

Plan
Grundriss
Niveau
Pianta

0 1 2

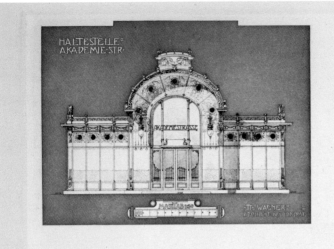

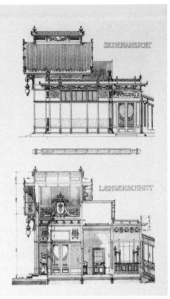

Elevation and sections
Élévation et sections

Aufriss und Schnitte
Prospetto e sezioni

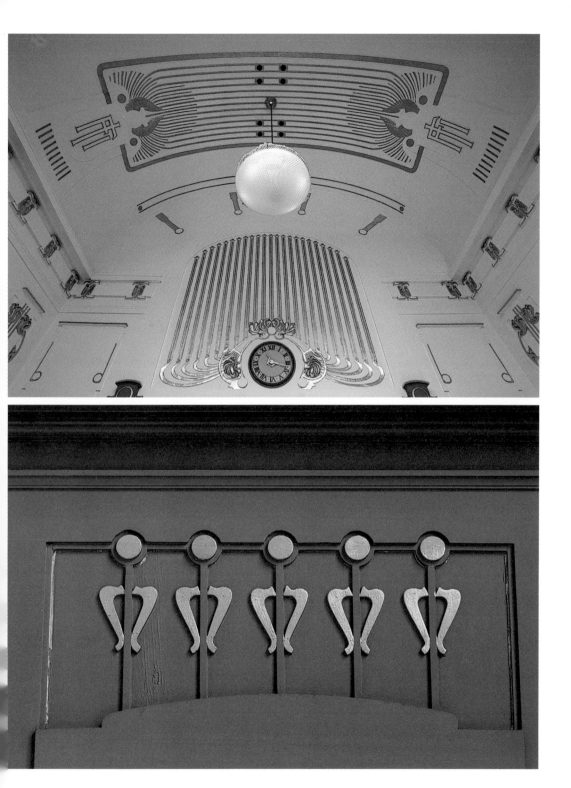

Steinhof Church

Baumgartner Höhe 1, Vienna, Austria
1902–1907

Otto Wagner won the competition for the development of the extensive project of which this church forms a part: the psychiatric complex at Steinhof. With this building, the architect was proposing the creation of a church for contemporary humanity. Situated at the highest point on the landscape, it dominates the whole project. The influences on this piece are highly varied in type: the framing is neoclassical, the spatial organization looks back toward the Renaissance, while the last suggestion is baroque. Thus, we find the work originating a wonderful play of forms, lights, and fields. The dome is faced in copper panels and suggests Balkan architecture. Representing the Secessionist movement, Kolo Moser's stained glass windows stand out, as do Remigius Jeiling's and Rudolf Jettmar's altar mosaics, Richard Luksch's statues, and the angels by Othmar Schimkowitz. Outside the building, the rubblework foundation contrasts with the marble panels. Inside again, the dome is closed by a vault comprised of a fine gilt netting with small white square panels. By taking the ceiling down 56 feet, the acoustics and heating problems were solved.

Otto Wagner gewann den Wettbewerb für ein Großprojekt, zu dem auch diese Kirche gehörte: die Niederösterreichische Landesnervenheilanstalt „Am Steinhof". Mit diesem Gebäude hatte es sich der Architekt zum Ziel gesetzt, eine Kirche für den modernen Menschen zu schaffen. Sie befindet sich auf dem höchsten Punkt der Umgebung und hebt sich so prächtig aus dem Gesamtkomplex heraus. Beim Bau sind verschiedene Einflüsse zu verzeichnen: Eine neoklassische Struktur und eine Raumaufteilung, die an Renaissance erinnert, während der Gesamteindruck barock ist. So entstand ein wundervolles Zusammenspiel aus Formen, Licht und Raum. Die Kuppel ist mit Kupfertafeln verkleidet und erinnert an die Architektur des Balkans. Die auffallendsten Elemente der Secessionsbewegung sind die Glasfenster von Kolo Moser, die Altarmosaiken von Remigius Jeiling und Rudolf Jettmar, die Statuen von Richard Luksch und die Engel des Pronaos von Othmar Schimkowitz. Das Fundament aus Mauerwerk steht außen zu den Marmorplatten im Gegensatz. Im Inneren des Gebäudes wird die Kuppel durch ein Gewölbe abgeschlossen, das aus einem Netz feiner, goldener Profile gebildet wird, die kleine, quadratische, weiße Tafeln tragen. Die Decke wurde um 17 m hinabgesenkt, so dass das Problem der Akustik und Beheizung gelöst war.

Otto Wagner gagna le concours pour le développement d'un grand projet dont cette église faisait partie : l'ensemble psychiatrique du Steinhof. Avec cette construction, l'architecte se proposait de bâtir une église pour l'homme de son temps. Située sur le point le plus élevé du paysage, elle domine orgueilleusement l'ensemble du projet. Les influences qu'elle reflète sont de diverses tendances : la structure est néoclassique, l'organisation de l'espace tend vers le style Renaissance, alors que la dernière touche est Baroque. Ceci provoque un merveilleux jeu de formes, de lumières et d'espaces. La coupole est revêtue de plaques de cuivre et rappelle les architectures balkaniques. En tant que témoins du mouvement « Sezession » on remarque les vitraux de Kolo Moser, les mosaïques des autels de Remigius Jeiling et Rudolf Jettmar, les statues de Richard Luksch et les anges du pronaos qui sont de Othmar Schimkowitz. A l'extérieur, le soubassement de maçonnerie contraste avec les plaques de marbre et à l'intérieur la coupole est fermée par une voûte constituée par un réseau de profilés dorés qui soutient des petits panneaux carrés de couleur blanche. En rabaissant le toit à 17 mètres on réussit à résoudre les problèmes d'acoustique et de chauffage.

Otto Wagner vinse il concorso per sviluppare un ampio progetto in cui la chiesa é una parte di questo: il complesso psichiatrico di Steinhof. Con questo edificio, l'architetto voleva raggiungere l'obiettivo di creare una chiesa per l'uomo moderno. Collocata nel punto più alto del paesaggio si distacca sobriamente dal complesso del progetto. Le influenze che riceve sono di diverse inclinazioni: la struttura é neoclassica, l'organizzazione dello spazio ricorda quello del Rinascimento, mentre l'ultima suggestione é barocca. Questo origina un magnifico gioco di forme, luci e spazi. La cupola é rivestita con pannelli di rame e ricorda l'architettura balcanica. Come rappresentazione del movimento secessionista, risaltano in modo particolare le vetrate di Kolo Moser, i mosaici degli altari di Remigius Jeiling e Rudolf Jettmar, le statue di Richard Luksch e gli angeli del pronao di Othmar Schimkowitz. Negli esterni, contrasta il basamento in muratura placcato di marmo, mentre all'interno la cupola viene chiusa da una volta costruita da una rete di profili dorati che regge piccoli pannelli di colore bianco. Dove il tetto diminuisce di altezza (17 metri) si sono risolti i problemi di acustica e di riscaldamento.

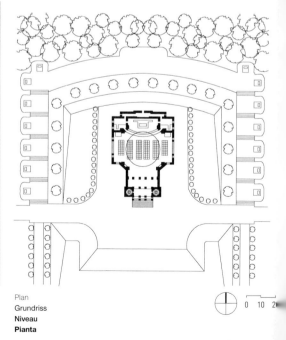

Plan
Grundriss
Niveau
Pianta

0 10 20

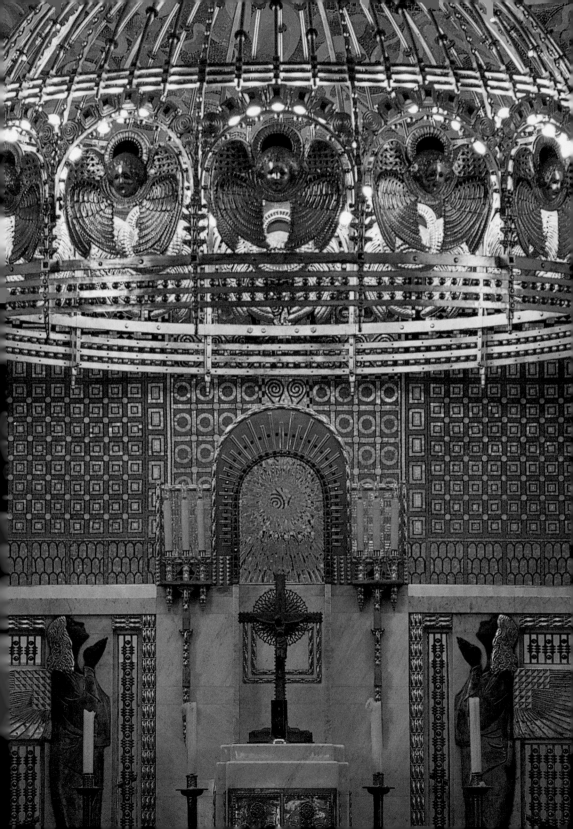

Postsparkasse of Austria

Georg-Coch-Platz 2, Vienna, Austria
1903–1912

In this building, the architectural legacies are not reflected in the same way as in Wagner's other works. Instead, they now represent the architecture of the new century. The aim of this building was clear because it was a new bank project and the architect wanted to present a container adequate to what it was to contain: money. The placement of the space, which stands out monumentally at one end of the square, does much to enable our appreciation of the column flanked by two attached figures that reign like two protective goddesses on high, the work of Schimkowitz. The whole work is faced in granite and marble panels studded with aluminum rivets. These latter elements are concentrated in greatest density on the central façade, as if to emphasize its presence. Aluminum was also used for the radiators, the entrance marquee, the pilasters of the main bay, and the statues. Once again, Wagner's personal language speaks in repeating spaces that ironize on architectural decoration. At a moment when the Secession was breaking up, Wagner's development showed him able to go beyond Art Nouveau and the baroque trend.

An diesem Gebäude ist das architektonische Erbe nicht so deutlich wie in anderen Werken Wagners zu erkennen, es repräsentiert vielmehr die neue Architektur und das neue Jahrhundert. Der Zweck dieses Gebäudes war ganz eindeutig, da es sich um den Entwurf für eine Bank handelte. Der Architekt wollte eine geeignete Umhüllung für das schaffen, was sich darin befinden würde, nämlich Geld. Durch die Lage des Gebäudes, das sich herrschaftlich hinten am Platz erhebt, kann man die Akroterien mit den beiden von Schimkowitz stammenden Figuren bewundern, die wie Schutzgötter von oben den Platz beherrschen. Das Gebäude ist mit Granit- und Marmorplatten verkleidet, die mit Aluminiumstiften befestigt und an der mittleren Fassade am dichtesten verlegt sind, was die Wirkung dieser Fassade noch unterstreicht. Auch die Heizkörper, die Markisen am Eingang, die Säulen im Saal und die Statuen sind aus Aluminium. Die persönliche Ausdrucksweise Wagners materialisiert sich hier noch einmal in Modulen, die sich wiederholen und die architektonische Zierelemente bilden. In der Zeit, als die Secession langsam auseinander fiel, entwickelte Wagner sich weiter und überwand die Art Nouveau und die barocken Tendenzen.

Dans cette construction, l'héritage architectural n'est pas aussi évident que dans les autres œuvres de Wagner, parce qu'il représente déjà la nouvelle architecture et le nouveau siècle. La finalité de ce nouvel édifice était bien claire puisqu'il s'agissait d'un projet de banque : l'architecte voulut représenter un ensemble rappelant un coffre, en adéquation avec ce qu'il allait contenir : de l'argent. La situation de l'ensemble, qui domine fièrement le fond de la place, permet d'apprécier les acrotères avec ses deux personnages, œuvres de Schimkowitz, qui règnent au sommet du bloc comme des déesses protectrices. L'ensemble a été revêtu de plaques de granit et de marbre, fixées par des boulons en aluminium, et placés avec la plus grande densité possible sur la façade centrale la soulignant ainsi. Les radiateurs, la marquise de l'entrée, les piliers de la salle et les statues ont aussi été construites en aluminium. Une fois de plus, le langage personnel de Wagner se concrétise en modules qui vont en se répétant et qui donnent leur formes aux décorations architecturales. Au moment où le mouvement Secession est en passe de se décomposer, Wagner démontre par son évolution qu'il dépasse l'Art Nouveau et la tendance baroque.

In questo edificio le eredità architettoniche non si riflettono così chiaramente come per le altre opere di Wagner, quanto invece rappresenta l'architettura del nuovo secolo. L'obiettivo di questo edificio era chiaro, considerato il fatto che il tema era una banca: l'architetto volle rappresentare un contenitore adeguato per poter contenere tutto il richiesto, soldi. Il volume, che si distacca fastuosamente dal fondo della piazza, permette di apprezzare i piedistalli con due figure che comandano come dee protettrici dall'alto, opera di Schimkowitz. Il complesso é stato rivestito da placche di granito e marmo fissate grazie a perni di allumino disposti con maggior intensità nella facciata centrale, per enfatizzarla. Dello stesso materiale vennero realizzati anche I radiatori, la pergola dell'ingresso, i pilastri della sala e le statue. Una volta ancora, il linguaggio personale di Wagner si materializza in moduli che si ripetono e che creano ornamento architettonico. Nel momento in cui la Secession di sta sfaldando, Wagner dimostra, durante tutta la sua evoluzione, il superamento dell'Art Nuveau e della tendenza barocca.

Entry perspective
Zeichnung des Eingangs
Perspective de l'entrée
Prospettiva dell'entrata

General perspective
Generalperspektive
Perspective de l'emsemble
Prospettiva generale

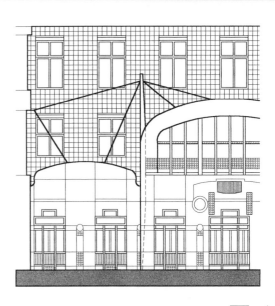

0 1 2

Residence at Neustiftgasse 40

Neustiftgasse 40, Vienna, Austria
1910

This building was planned ten years after those on the Linke Wienzeile. The comparison shows how Wagner's last projects could be even more radical than those of his youth. The only exterior ornamentation is a course in blue glazed brick framing different floors and the sign on which the street address is inscribed in capital letters. Straight lines also prevail inside the piece, in the halls and the stairway. A series of straight-lined drawings cover the walls and the ceilings, filling the empty space and creating very pure spaces. The materials and colors used inside contribute to the creation of this cold feel: marble, metal in gray, blue, or white tones. The architect, the building's owner, took up residence in one of the apartments for city use. In these very well-lighted apartments, austerity and elegance intermingle to give rise to an anxiously awaited architectural progress. These are the first manifestations of rationalism.

Otto Wagner entwarf dieses Gebäude zehn Jahre nach denen in der Linken Wienzeile. Wenn man seine letzten Werke mit den ersten vergleicht, erkennt man, dass sie noch radikaler als die seiner Jugendzeit sind. Die einzige Dekoration außen am Gebäude, die zu sehen ist, ist ein Streifen aus blau verglasten Ziegeln, der mehrere Wohnungen umrahmt und ein Schild, auf dem in Großbuchstaben die Adresse zu finden ist, an der sich das Haus befindet. Auch im Inneren, in den Fluren und im Treppenhaus überwiegen die geraden Linien. Eine Reihe geradliniger Zeichnungen schmückt die Wände und die Decken. Sie füllen die Leere und erschaffen einen Ort großer Reinheit. Die Materialien und Farben, die im Inneren des Gebäudes verwendet wurden, tragen zu diesem kalten Aussehen noch bei: Marmor, Metall in Grau-, Blau- oder Weißtönen. Der Architekt, der auch der Eigentümer des Gebäudes war, bezog eine der Wohnungen als Stadtresidenz. In diesen sehr klar angelegten Wohnungen mischen sich Nüchternheit und Eleganz, um so eine bereits sehnsüchtig erwartete Entwicklung vorwegzunehmen, den Rationalismus.

Otto Wagner fit le projet de ce complexe dix ans après ceux de Linke Wienzeile. La comparaison montre comment ses derniers travaux pouvaient être encore plus osés que ceux des jeunes de ce temps. L'unique décoration extérieure qui apparaît est une frange de briques vitrifiées de couleur bleue qui encadre plusieurs étages et la plaque écrite en majuscules indiquant l'adresse où se trouve l'immeuble. A l'intérieur, les lignes droites dominent, tout comme dans les couloirs et dans les escaliers. Une série de dessins rectilignes habillent les murs et les plafonds en comblant les vides créant ainsi des espaces d'une grande pureté. Les matériaux et couleurs qui furent employés à l'intérieur contribuèrent à créer cet aspect froid : marbre, métal dans les tons gris, bleus ou blancs. L'architecte – propriétaire de l'immeuble – prit un des appartements pour en faire sa résidence en ville. Dans ces logements très lumineux, la sobriété se mêle à l'élégance pour laisser place à un progrès architectural attendu avec impatience ; ce sont les premières manifestations du rationalisme.

Otto Wagner progettò questo complesso dieci anni dopo la proposta di Linke Wienzeile. Il paragone mostra come gli ultimi lavori potevano essere ancora più radicali ripsetto a quelli giovanili. L'unica decorazione esterna che era concessa era una stricia di mattoni smaltati di colore azzurro hanno la funzione di fasce di marcapiano tra i vari livelli, e un'etichetta su cui si scrive l'indirizzo dell'edificio, scritto in caratteri maiuscoli. Le linee rette prevalgono all'interno, nei corridoi e nelle scale. Una serie si disegni rettilinei vestono le pareti e i tetti riempiendo così i vuoti e creando sapzi di gran purezza. I materiali e i colori utilizzati all'interno contribuiscono a creare questo aspetto freddo: marmo, metallo con tonalità di grigi, azzurri o biavo. L'architetto, proprietario dell'edificio, prese una degli appartamenti come sua residenza cittadina. In questi alloggi di grandissima chiarezza, sembra mescolarsi la sobrietà e l'eleganza per lasciare spazioa un progresso architettonico affannosamente sperato; sono le prime manifestazioni del razionalismo.

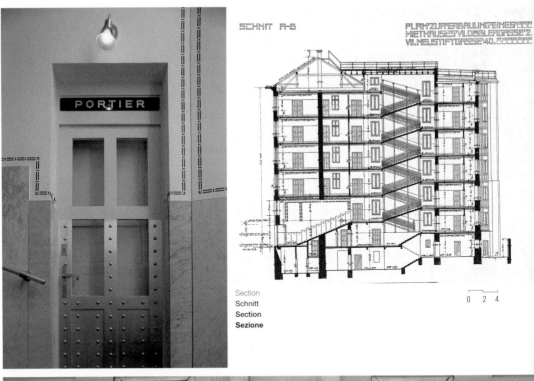

SCHNIT A-B

PLAN·ZUR·ERBAUUNG·EINES·
MIETHAUSES·VII.DÖBLERGASSE·2.
VII.NEUSTIFTGASSE·40.

Section
Schnitt
Section
Sezione

0 2 4

74 Residence at Neustiftgasse 40

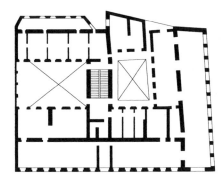

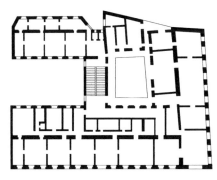

Ground floor
Erdgeschoss
Rez-de-chaussée
Piano terra

First floor
Erstes Obergeschoss
Premier étage
Primo piano

0   2   4

Chronology of Otto Wagner's works

1841	Otto Wagner is born in Penzig, Vienna, Austria.
1857–1863	Wagner studies at the Wiener Polytechnisches Institut and the Königliche Bauakademie in Berlin. He frequents the Akademie der Bildenden Künste of Vienna, where his teachers include the planners of the Vienna Opera.
1863	Kursalon competition, Stadtpark, Vienna, Austria.
1865	Wasagasse Theater, Vienna, Austria.
1869	Rental house at Bellariastraße 4, Vienna, Austria.
1870	Synagogue in Budapest, Hungary.
1874	Grabenhof, Vienna, Austria.
1877	Block of apartments and offices at Schottenring 23, Vienna, Austria.
1878	Reconstruction of the Dilanabad, Vienna, Austria.
1879	Project for a church, Soborsin, Hungary.
1880	Competition for Artibus ideas for a museum neighborhood, Vienna, Austria.
1881	Rental houses at Rathausstraße 3, Vienna, Austria.
	Studio for a Goethe monument, Vienna, Austria.
1883	Rental house at Stadiongasse 6-8, Vienna, Austria.
1884	Länderbank (competition 1882), Vienna, Austria.
	Rental house at Lobkowitzplatz 1, Vienna, Austria.
1886	Hahn House, Baden, Germany.
	Project for the Russian Embassy, Vienna, Austria.
	Wagner Villa at Hüttelbergstraße 26, Vienna, Austria.
1888	Rental house at Universitätstraße 12, Vienna, Austria.
1890	Project for a parish church in Esseg.
1891	Wagner House (later Hoyos Palace) at Rennweg 3, Vienna, Austria.
	Rental house at Rennweg 1, Vienna, Austria.
1892–1893	Competition for the general regulatory plan of Vienna and reclassification of the Stubenviertel Vienna, Austria.
1893	Project for the Ministry of Commerce, Vienna, Austria.
1894	Family burial crypt, Innsbruck, Austria.
1894–1901	Vienna Metro Stations, Austria. 35 stations, bridges, and viaducts.
1894–1908	Reordering work on the Donaukanal; Nussdorf dam with flood administration buildings.
1895	Johannes-Kapelle at the Gürtel, Vienna, Austria.
	Anker House at the Graben, Vienna, Austria.
1896	First project for the Fernando Bridge, Vienna, Austria.
1898	Wagner-Zimmer in the Jubiläums-Ausstellung, Vienna, Austria.
	Project for the new Fine Arts Academy, Vienna, Austria.
	Hofpavillon, Schönbrunn, Austria.
	Karlsplatz, Vienna, Austria.
	Project for the re-zoning of the Capucine church and the imperial crypt, Vienna, Austria.
1898–1899	The Linke Wienzeile Building, rental residence at Linke Wienzeile 38, Vienna, Austria.
	Majolica House, Vienna, Austria.
1900	Administration pavilion for the royal gardens at the International World Exposition, Paris, France

	"Agitationsprojekt" for Kaiser Franz Joseph, Stadtmuseum at the Karlsplatz, Vienna, Austria.
1902	Sub-post office Die Zeit (not conserved), Vienna, Austria.
1902–1907	Steinhof Church, Vienna, Austria.
1903	Project for reform work on the Karlsplatz, Vienna, Austria.
	Project for a monumental fountain on the Karlsplatz, Vienna, Austria.
	New project for the Stadtmuseum, Vienna, Austria.
	Project for an exhibition hall for the Museum of Applied Arts, Vienna, Austria.
1903–1912	Postsparkasse of Austria, Vienna, Austria.
1904	Project for a building for the large stores on the Karlsplatz, Vienna, Austria.
	Study for Vindobona Bridge, Vienna, Austria.
1904–1908	Kaiserbad dam with the control building.
1905	Reform project for the entrance to the Naschmarkt, Vienna, Austria.
	Project for the Interimskirche, Vienna, Austria.
	Second project for a monumental fountain on the Karlsplatz, Vienna, Austria.
	Two projects for the Fernando Bridge, Vienna, Austria.
1906	Project and variation for the Wiener Gesellschaft Palace, Vienna, Austria.
1907	First project for the Zedlitz Gallery, Vienna, Austria.
	New project and variation for the Stadtmuseum, Vienna, Austria.
1908	Project for the House of Glory, Vienna, Austria.
	Second project for the Ministry of Commerce, Vienna, Austria.
1909	Competition for the Technical Museum, Vienna, Austria.
	Project for the Stadtmuseum in Schmelz, Vienna, Austria.
1910	Residence at Neustiftgasse 40, Vienna, Austria.
	First project for the University Library, Vienna, Austria.
	Second project for the new Academy of Fine Arts, Vienna, Austria.
	Project for a hotel in Ring, Vienna, Austria.
	New project for the Stadtmuseum, Vienna, Austria.
1910–1913	Lupusheilstätte, Vienna, Austria.
1911	Plan for District 22 and unlimited expansion plan for Vienna, Austria.
1912	Project for a competition for the Stadtmuseum, Vienna, Austria.
	Rental residences at Döblergasse 4, Vienna, Austria.
1912–1913	Wagner Villa at Hüttelbergstrasse 28, Vienna, Austria.
	Second project for the Zedlitz Gallery, Vienna, Austria.
	Project for Art of the Twentieth Century, Vienna, Austria.
1914	Second project for the University Library, Vienna, Austria.
	Project for the Palmschloss Sanatorium, Bresanone, Italy.
1915	Project for barracks for convalescing soldiers, Vienna, Austria.
	Project for the Sankt-Magdalenen-Spital, Vienna, Austria.
1916	Project for an equestrian monument, Vienna, Austria.
1917	Project for the reconstruction of the Brigittabrücke, Vienna, Austria.
	Project for the House of the Child, Vienna, Austria.
1918	Otto Wagner dies.

Credits

Drawings in the specified pages were taken from the following institutions:

© Historisches Museum der Stadt Wien, in pages 6, 7, 15, 20, 25, 52, 58 above, 66 left and 75;

© Austrian National Library, Bildarchiv, in pages 5, 8, 12, 25 below, 28, 58, 66 right, 72 and backcover.